The Complete Book on Cat Behavior

To my father, Larry Vidinha, whose love
For cats I will always cherish

By Gwen Bohnenkamp

About The Author

Gwen Bohnenkamp is an internationally recognized author and behaviorist. As President of Perfect Paws, Inc. in San Francisco, Gwen provided training and consultation services to pet owners, veterinarians and humane associations throughout the United States and Canada. As Vice President of The Center for Applied Animal Behavior in Berkeley California, she co-authored a series of behavior booklets with veterinarian Dr. Ian Dunbar. At the San Francisco SPCA, Gwen founded and directed the largest and most comprehensive animal behavior correction program in the United States. She established and implemented the San Francisco SPCA's Animal Behavior Hotline, the country's first call-in animal behavior correction service.

During her career, Gwen has spoken on the topic of animal behavior for numerous local, civic and professional organizations, including the Commonwealth Club of California. Gwen has appeared in a variety of media including TV (where she had her own segment titled "Pet Calls"), newspaper and magazine (People Magazine, Ladies Home Journal, Better Homes and Gardens, TV Guide); and for over eight years appeared on Northern California's most popular news-talk radio station, answering questions on animal behavior. She instructed a course on Applied Animal Behavior at San Francisco State University and is the author of From the Cat's Point of View; Kitty Kassettes; Help! My Dog Has an Attitude; Manners for the Modern Dog and Raising Kaylee.

*Special thanks
to the following for their inspiration,
encouragement and assistance:
My husband John,
Kimberly Karr-Warner, Amy Shapiro,
Ronn Owens, Dr. Ian Dunbar, Dr. Michael W. Fox.*

Illustrations by Robert Eames
Layout and Design by John Simon

Library of Congress No. 3-080-384
ISBN 0-9644601-1-4

Published by
PERFECT PAWS Publishing
fax: 650-745-2647
email: discount@perfectpaws.com
website: www.perfectpaws.com

Contents

This chapter provides the foundation for understanding why your cat behaves as he does. Once you understand the hows and whys of kitty's behavior, you can effectively address and resolve any problem using the 5-step approach described here.

Discover the territorial nature of the cat and how scent plays a vital role in kitty's behavior. Using this knowledge, you can help bring a new cat into your home with the least amount of stress; learn how to best move with your cat; find tips on how to bring another cat home; and how to deal with a fearful, nervous cat.

Everything you need to know about how to train or retrain your kitty to use her litterbox. Understand why cats refuse to use their box so you can avoid the common pitfalls before a problem is created. This chapter also addresses territorial scent marking or spraying.

Contents

Introduction

Most of what we think are behavior problems or misbehavior in cats are actually perfectly normal and natural cat behaviors. The cat that bounces off the ceiling and climbs the walls at 3 in the morning is normal. Cats are nocturnal. The cat that shreds the living room furniture is also normal. Cats need to scratch. It helps if we can understand why cats do the things they do from the cat's viewpoint and not attribute human motivations to them.

Cats will often urinate in your house because of their strong territorial instinct, not because they are vindictive. They claw your furniture because they need to condition their nails, not because they are spiteful or just causing trouble.

This book is going to explain what is normal behavior in cats and how we can still let them act like cats, but in a way we can live with. We can't have cats terrorizing us and keeping us up all night, and I don't think anyone wants their cat to destroy their furniture. It's not fair to have a cat and expect her to act like a dog, or a person, or anything other than a cat. It's not fair and it is also not possible. We don't punish birds for singing and we don't say to our dogs, "No tail-wagging allowed!"

So instead of telling our cat that he is not allowed to scratch or run crazy through the house, let's find out how we can redirect these behaviors to outlets that are acceptable. Let's set up an environment and lifestyle that meets our cat's needs as well as our own. Instead of forcing and punishing cats into being something they are not, let's treat them, understand them and respect them as cats.

Let's take a look at cat behavior from the cat's point of view.......

1

No Bad Cats

Diagnosis

When a cat owner comes to me with a behavior problem, there are five general considerations I take into account.

1. Communication. How are the owner and the cat interacting with one another?

2. The Holistic Approach. Is the cat getting enough attention and exercise?

3. The Realistic Approach. Does the cat have outlets for his normal behavior?

4. Prevention. Can the problem be prevented?

5. Medical. Is there a medical cause for the behavior?

Let's look at these in more detail.

Who's Misbehaving ?

One of the first questions I ask is how are the owner and cat communicating. Many owners look at their cats as little humans in furry suits who understand English. They set their cat in their laps and try to explain why she shouldn't scratch the stereo speakers.

Problems often arise simply because the owners don't realize what they are communicating to their cat and don't understand what their cat is trying to tell them. Cats don't inherently understand English. But they do understand consequences of their actions. They learn by experience. The easiest way to communicate with and teach a cat is through immediate reward for good behavior and negative consequences for misbehavior. It is really very simple. You reward good behavior. You reprimand bad behavior. But, in day to day living, it is often difficult to apply this simple principle.

For example, you just get home from a hard day's work. You plop down on the couch to relax and watch the evening news. Then suddenly, the cat springs out of nowhere, nips you on the ankle and tears out down the hall. Likewise, you jump up and chase the cat down the hall, screaming and maybe even trying to squirt him with a plant sprayer. You think you're showing displeasure and reprimanding the cat, but let's look at it from kitty's point of view.

Kitty has been home alone all day, bored stiff. You come home and act like a giant slug. The cat wants some stimulation and attention and has found the perfect way to get some action. To the cat, this is a fun and rewarding game. So without even knowing it, you have unintentionally rewarded your cat for this obnoxious behavior. Both you and the cat have misunderstood and miscommunicated with each other.

Another example is when a cat owner comes home and finds a puddle on the floor. The owner grabs the cat, yells, rubs her nose in the urine then throws the cat in the litterbox. The owner thinks he is teaching the cat that she is supposed to use the litterbox, but the only thing the cat is learning is that the owner is a deranged maniac! Sometimes the owner comes home and is loving and affectionate, but other times he comes home and is violent and aggressive. All this does is develop mistrust, fear and insecurity in the cat.

When cats feel insecure, anxious or stressed, they will often express their anxiety by eliminating outside the litterbox. If the owner does not evaluate this behavior but immediately punishes the cat for not using the litterbox, a vicious cycle develops. The more the cat is punished, the more stressed he becomes. The more stressed he becomes, the more he doesn't use his litterbox. The worse the litterbox problems gets, the more the cat is punished. Instead of punishment, find ways to reduce the cat's stress level and concentrate on rewarding good behavior.

In fact, reward for good behavior alone often solves most behavior problems. A woman called me complaining that her cat named Robert was frequently not using his box. She said she would occasionally see him use it, but most of the time he would go some place else. Her carpets were ruined and needed to be completely replaced. She punished him, but only if she caught him in the act. She insisted he knew he was being bad.

Naturally she was hesitant when I told her to stop the punishment completely and instead she should go overboard rewarding and praising him on those few times she saw him use his box. I finally convinced her to try it since her methods were not working and the problem certainly could not get worse. She finally promised to buy some fresh salmon to reward Robert when he used his box.

A few weeks later, I received a phone call. An enthusiastic voice at the other end simply said, "Robert has learned ballet!" It was Friday night ... was this someone who'd had a few drinks and dialed the wrong phone number? "Excuse me, but I think you have the wrong number. I don't know anyone named Robert, but I'm happy to hear he's taking ballet lessons." Then she reminded me that Robert was the cat who ruined her carpets. "OK," I thought, "but what does this have to do with ballet, and shouldn't she be calling Hollywood instead of me?"

Then she told me that it didn't take long for Robert to realize that the special treats came only when she saw him use the litterbox. So, every time he was about to use his box, he would do a little "ballet" dance across the room and gracefully land in his box. He wanted to be absolutely sure he got her attention so he would be sure to get his treat. The litterbox problem had been corrected with the exclusive use of reward.

Jump Or Else

It is often difficult to think of training without the use of reprimands. Imagine trying to train a dolphin to jump through a hoop. I can hear it now, "Jump, or I'll swat you on the nose with a newspaper!" It just would not work. This is also true of cats. You cannot train a cat by making him feel guilty; you can't threaten them, dominate them, force or punish them.

If you want to train a cat, you have to find the right motivation to lure and entice kitty into obeying. If you say, "Cat, get over here or I'll twist your neck," the cat is simply going to run the other way. But if you say, "Come here kitty," and wave half a salmon in her face, no doubt she will come running.

I rarely recommend the use of reprimand, but if appropriate, it must be done correctly or it will only make the problem worse. Reprimands should never be used with litterbox problems. You'll learn more about this in chapter three.

Let Me Count The Ways

The worst consequences of reprimands come from the use of delayed punishment. By that I mean you punish the cat for something she has done either a few hours ago or even a few seconds ago. Whatever your cat is doing at the exact moment you punish her, that is what she will associate the punishment with. If you come home and find your cat has scratched your curtains or chairs, and you punish her then, she will learn to be afraid of you entering your home and will probably stop running up to greet you.

You're in the kitchen. You hear raking noises in your living room and go running in to scream at your cat; but you arrive half a second late. You scream at kitty for scratching the chair just when she is leaving the chair. Whatever your cat believes she is being punished for, it is not for the behavior you were trying to correct - scratching the chair - because that is not what she was doing when you came in and started yelling.

If you point to the claw marks and scold her, she may think, "What's wrong? Aren't they long enough, or deep enough?"

Another consequence of punishment is that the cat will associate it with you. Even if you catch kitty in the act of the crime, it does not stop the behavior, it just teaches kitty not to do these things in front of you. He will just wait until you leave the room or house.

One client of mine punished her cat for scratching the furniture. The cat knew he would get in trouble if he was caught scratching so whenever he heard her coming, he would dash off and hide. But he would also dash off and hide if he heard her coming when he was scratching his own post. He was simply afraid to scratch anything in front of her.

The most important aspect of training a cat is to praise and reward him for doing the right thing. But if the cat won't do these things in front of you, how in the world are you going to praise and reward him?

Remember, reprimands and punishment should rarely be used with cats. They don't respond well to it and it usually only makes matters worse. However, we can discourage our cats from doing certain things by making items or places undesirable, while at the same time making appropriate things rewarding.

For example, if you don't want your cat to scratch the couch, you can temporarily turn it into something he doesn't want to scratch until the habit is broken and he has learned to use his own scratching post. Your cat will avoid the couch because he doesn't like the couch. It has nothing to do with you. The cat won't scratch it whether you are there or not. This is discussed in more detail in the chapter on scratching furniture.

Catcersize

The second general consideration when solving a behavior problem is what I call the holistic approach. Many problems are caused by the cat's excess energy. This is especially true of young cats. Their energy has to be vented somewhere. Often you will see cats chasing phantom spirits, climbing walls, jumping from counter top to table top, knocking things off and breaking them. They will steal, chew on and even hide your socks or the kitchen sink sponge. Unfortunately, sometimes they will even chew or lick themselves raw as a nervous habit. These are things that cats do. You can't expect them to knit in front of the fireplace, do the Zumba aerobic workout or invite the guys over for a hand of poker.

To vent this energy, set aside a daily play session with your cat. Give him fun and active things to do. The object is to devote 100% of your attention to the cat during these regular play sessions.

It doesn't necessarily have to be a lengthy play session, and it doesn't have to be that active. With some cats, it is enough to just spend some quality time together. What is important is that the time spent together must be quality time.

Your cat needs something to look forward to on a regular and consistent basis. If you have an active, energetic cat, then the longer the session and the more active it is, the more energy the cat will vent. A tired, happy cat won't have the energy to get into trouble. The chapter on hyperactive and destructive behavior will give you some ideas of games you can play with your cat.

In addition, proper diet, nutrition, good health and regular veterinary check-ups are important to maintaining a happy cat.

It's The Real Thing

The third general consideration in solving a behavior problem is what I call the realistic approach. Cats have certain needs and it's up to you to provide for them or your cat will do her own thing.

Instead of stopping a particular behavior altogether, the realistic approach is getting the behavior under control. We understand that cats need to eat and eliminate. Just because she may raid our lunch box or pee in the closet, we don't say the cat is not allowed to eat again or cork the cat so she won't eliminate. Instead, we give her cat food and provide a litterbox.

This idea of providing for the cat's needs extends to all of their needs. If we don't want the cat to scratch our furniture, we don't say, "No scratching allowed - ever." Instead, we should provide and teach the cat to use her own scratching post. If the cat likes plants, then we should provide her with her own kitty garden and make our house plants off-limits.

The realistic approach recognizes that the cat is going to act like a cat, but you can teach her to act in ways that are acceptable in your home. It is unfair and practically impossible to stop certain behaviors, so let's just get them under control.

Just Say No

The fourth general consideration is prevention. This

is the single most important aspect of behavior training; and the most important thing you can do is to prevent bad habits from developing in the first place. When a habit is formed, it is difficult to stop. If a habit is prevented from forming then you don't have to try to break it.

If you never smoked a cigarette, then you wouldn't have the problem of being addicted to them and you wouldn't have to go through the torture and agony of quitting.

One way to prevent bad habits from forming and also a method of breaking already established habits is through the use of confinement. Confinement is no different than putting a baby in a play pen. When mom is cooking dinner in the kitchen and can't watch baby, she puts him in a playpen so he stays out of trouble and doesn't get hurt. She doesn't expect the baby to know that the stove is hot or that he could fall down the stairs. She doesn't expect the baby to stay out of trouble without supervision. Why do we expect more from our cats than we do from our own children? We want them to read our minds and automatically know what they should and shouldn't do.

The playpen is not a jail. When children get used to it, they learn to entertain themselves and enjoy their playpen. That's why they're called playpens. When you confine your cat, you should have the same attitude. Make it a special place for your cat. You should consider it the cat's playroom.

Make the room a pleasant and fun place to be. Introduce it slowly and gradually, spend time there with your cat until he feels confident in his own special haven. Don't just toss kitty in and walk away. Give your cat things to do in there. Cats really don't mind being confined. After all, how many times have you looked for your kitty only to find her curled up in a dresser drawer that you left open? Cats love to hide in boxes, paper bags and hang out on the top shelf of the linen closet. Now these spaces are really confined. You are going to give your cat much more space than that.

The cat is not going to be confined forever; just until she can be trusted to have full freedom of the house. Part of confinement is prevention. You may as well prevent having your entire house become a huge litterbox while the cat is being litterbox-trained. Until our human babies are potty trained, we put diapers on them to prevent accidents. With children, we are very prevention oriented, so why shouldn't we be that way with our cats?

Confinement is prevention, but equally as important, confinement also helps the cat develop good habits. If the only available scratching item in the playroom is a scratching post, then kitty will develop a habit of scratching it simply because there is nothing else there to scratch on. The more the cat scratches the post, the stronger that habit becomes. The longer the cat is prevented from scratching a couch, the more likely that habit will be broken.

There are three purposes for confinement. First, it protects your property. Your cat cannot scratch your couch because the couch is not in the cat's playroom. Second, it protects your cat. Kitty doesn't know that plants and chemicals can be poisonous and that electric cords can kill. Third, it allows the development of good habits while at the same time breaks and prevents bad habits from forming.

In order to accomplish these three things, the cat's playroom should not have anything in it that you don't want destroyed; it should not have anything in it that can harm the cat; it should not have anything in it that you don't want the cat to develop a habit of eating, scratching, soiling, playing with, sleeping on or whatever. It should have lots of toys, two or more scratching/climbing posts, bedding, a litterbox, food and water bowls. This is the cat's playroom, not a jail. It is only temporary until kitty can be trusted to have full run of your home.

Preventing problem behavior is far easier than curing it. The earlier you can help your cat establish good habits, the better.

Drink Some Milk ...
Call Me In The Morning

The fifth general consideration is your cat's health. Proper diet, nutrition, exercise, play, and regular veterinary check-ups are essential to the cat's well-being. Any abnormal behavior or any sudden change in behavior should be checked out by your veterinarian as soon as possible.

You know how you sometimes get cranky or irritable when you have a headache. If you don't feel well, you usually aren't your normal self. If your stomach is upset, you may be visiting the human litterbox more frequently.

If you spend time with your cat and get to know him, you will notice changes in his behavior and habits right away. If there is a sudden change, don't assume your cat is just being a brat. Check with your veterinarian first. If kitty gets a clean bill of health, then look at it from the behavioral viewpoint.

Summary

These are the first five general areas I look into whenever I consult with an owner/cat client.

1. Communication. Cats learn by action and experience. Most problems are solved by rewarding and praising good behavior. Reprimands usually make the problem worse.

2. Holistic Approach. Cats need mental and physical exercise as well as quality attention and affection. A well-exercised and satisfied cat will not have to relieve stress, excess energy and boredom in ways you don't appreciate.

3. Realistic Approach. This is redirecting the cat's normal behavior to outlets that are acceptable to you in your home, but are also enjoyable for the cat.

4. Prevention. Preventing problem behavior is far easier than trying to cure it. The earlier and sooner you can help your cat establish good habits, the better.

5. Medical. Make sure that a physical condition is not causing the cat to misbehave.

2

Understanding Your Cat

Let's look at normal cat behavior. If we accept cats as cats and understand why they do what they do, it's more likely that we can live more comfortably with them and they with us. Problems arise when we superimpose our values and expectations on them.

We certainly don't want our cat to destroy our belongings and I'm sure cats don't want to endure the things we do to them when they do destroy our belongings. The cat doesn't enjoy punishment anymore than we enjoy the destruction of our new furniture.

When owners don't understand why their cats scratch their furniture or pee outside the litterbox, they lose their temper and punish the cat. This only serves to vent the owner's anger. Owners always tell me that the cat knows he been bad. This supposedly justifies the punishment. Whether the cat knows he's been bad or not, the punishment does nothing to cure the problem.

First, we should understand why cats do certain things, then take a look at how we can effectively cure the problem instead of wasting our time traumatizing the cat and finally in frustration getting rid of him when the problem doesn't go away.

I Smell Trouble

A cat's territorial instinct is so strong that it is the cause of most problem behavior. Problems range from urine-marking to scratching furniture to hiding under your bed for days and even to fighting.

Cats identify their territory through scent. This begins almost from birth. Cats are born deaf and blind, but as tiny kittens, they already have a keen sense of smell. When kittens are nursing on mom cat and you pull them all away from her, the kittens will all crawl back and find their own personal nipple every time. They can do this because each nipple has a unique smell and the kittens find it by it's special scent. If you pull the kittens away and wash mom's tummy off, and therefore any smells; the kittens come back all confused and will even start fighting because they can't find their personal milk dispenser.

So much of a cat's behavior is related to smell and their sense of territory. They identify their territory through smell. Their territory can be anything from mom's nipple, other cats or dogs, and people they live with, to objects and furniture that belong in the house where they live.

Many owners with two or more cats that are usually close friends will tell me that one cat will hiss and even fight with their best friend every time he comes back from the veterinarian's office. This is because the returning cat often doesn't smell the same - at least temporarily. The cat that stayed home doesn't recognize her friend when he comes home because he smells different. It's like a new cat is invading the territory.

You can help prevent this by understanding why it happens. When the returning cat is ready to come home, you can wipe him down with a scent that is familiar to the cat that stayed home. What usually works best is a towel that the cat has been sleeping on at home for a few days, or a part of his bedding. You can use some of your own clothing that has retained your scent. The idea is to make both cats feel secure by using a scent with which they are both familiar and comfortable.

Anything new, whether it's a new cat, a person coming to live or visit, or even a new chair can be considered an invasion of the cat's territory. I knew a cat that always sprayed urine on the mail when it was delivered through the door slot. Here was something that came flying into the cat's territory, so the cat had to put his mark on it. Perhaps kitty thought he was helping the owner out by stamping "Received" on it.

Cats are so territorial that they often prefer the company of familiar surroundings instead of their owner's company. It's well known that when owners move with a cat, the cat frequently returns or tries to return to his old home.

When I was in college in Illinois, every couple of semesters we used to like to change apartments and live somewhere new. Many of the rental properties came with cats. When we signed the rental agreement, part of the contract was taking care of the cat. When the time came for us to move, no matter how much we loved the cat, the cat had to stay. Kitty came with the territory!

It's difficult for us to understand how important smell is to the cat because we rely so much on sight and sound. The cat has a specialized scent organ that is located in the roof of the mouth just behind the upper front teeth. It is highly sensitive and when we see a cat use it, it looks like the cat is sneering and in a trance. Kitty raises his head slightly, draws back his upper lip and slightly opens his mouth. His tongue flickers inside or licks the roof of his mouth as he concentrates on getting a good whiff.

When your cat grooms herself, it is often related to scent and territory. We usually think of grooming as a cat just cleaning herself. But it has many functions. Licking keeps the cat's coat waterproof by stimulating oil glands. Licking also smooths the fur out so that it can be a better insulator, helping the cat keep warm when it's cold. Evaporation of saliva helps cool the cat off when it's hot. Licking of their sun-warmed fur also provides them with vitamin D. Licking can be a displacement activity when the cat is irritated, agitated, stressed or confused.

Grooming or licking helps the cat freshen up her own scent. Cats will rub up against people, other animals and objects to leave her scent on them and to remind her that they belong. But just as important, after she has rubbed up against something, (usually you, your dog or another cat) she licks herself to taste, smell and identify whatever she rubbed up against. When you see two cats grooming each other, the primary purpose is not mutual hygiene, but it is how they develop a close social bond.

No Trespassing

Cats are very territorial, but so are we. We put up signs and fences on and around our property. We put locks on our doors and alarms on our cars because these things are our property and territory. We want to feel secure in them and keep invaders out. We consider this normal human behavior, but when a cat expresses his territorial nature, we get all upset and immediately jump to conclusions. "The cat is being spiteful! He's angry. He's trying to get back at us, he must be jealous."

And I suppose if cats could talk, they would jump to some wrong conclusions about us too. If they saw us putting up a fence to keep the neighborhood kids out of our yard, the cat would probably laugh at us and think, "Look at those silly humans building a fence. Why don't they just go out and urine-mark along the property line?"

Cats and humans are different animals and do things in different ways. It is important to understand why cats do what they do. We want them to live in our society so we should help them adjust to our way of living instead of punishing them for acting like cats. They can't help doing what they do, after all, they are cats, not humans.

There are three basic ways that cats mark their territory. They rub up against things to leave their scent. This helps them identify their territory. It makes them feel more at home, whether they are rubbing up against you or the refrigerator. This type of marking is usually not a problem. In fact, everyone I know actually enjoys it. The other two ways that a cat marks its territory is what drives owners to drink, call me for advice, or get rid of the cat. These are urine-marking and scratching/clawing furniture. These behaviors will be discussed in later chapters.

Welcome Home Kitty

It is important to recognize the cat's strong sense of territory when bringing home a new cat or when moving to a new home. The most important thing you can do is help the cat adjust to his new territory.

The cat will undoubtedly be highly stressed because he is moving from one territory to another. The environment and smells he is used to will be gone and all the new smells will make the cat feel uncomfortable.

The smaller the territory that the cat has to become familiar with, the quicker he will adjust. If you are bringing a new cat home for the first time, find a quiet room and shut all the doors and windows. If brought in a carrier, set it down in a corner, open it up and just sit down across the room. Don't pull the cat out and smother him with attention. If the cat wants your affection, let him come to you for it. He may not want to come out of the box at all.

If that's the case, don't force him. On the other hand, he may jump right out, immediately run and hide under the bed or a chair. If he does, just leave him alone. Keep the room quiet and keep your distance from the cat. Just go about doing your business. You can talk quietly to yourself or even play some soft music, but ignore kitty. He needs time to watch what's going on and to adjust to the new sounds and smells.

Set his room up with a litterbox near his hiding place. Put his food and water bowls nearby but not close to his litterbox. Set up his scratching posts and scatter a few toys around. If this is a new cat, then he also needs time to get to know you. Don't rush him or force him. I know you're dying to make friends and you want to hug and cuddle with him, but he may not be ready for that.

The best thing you can do is let him get acquainted with you in his own time. Don't take it personally if he isn't sitting in your lap as soon as you'd like. Cats just need time and the more you try to rush it, the longer it will take.

Stray Cat

I worked with one client who took in a stray cat she found living in a stockroom where she worked. We knew nothing of his background. She set up his home in a guest room and every day went in to feed him and clean his litterbox. It took months before he would even poke his head out from under the bed to look at her. In fact, until this happened she wasn't even sure there was a cat there except that the food was gone every morning and the litterbox was dirty.

When he showed his face, she was so encouraged that she approached him to say hello. He hissed and scooted right back under the bed. It took another two weeks before he had the courage to poke his head out again. When he finally did, this time she just ignored him. She began to spend more time in his room, reading, listening to the stereo, talking on the phone. All this time the cat just watched her.

Another couple of weeks went by and he actually came out, sniffed her leg, rubbed up against it for half a second and zoomed back under the bed. She kept ignoring him while he kept coming out and staying a little longer each time before dashing away.

Next, we decided she could sit on the floor and spread a few tasty treats around her. Now when he came out, he would also find the special treats. So just as we predicted, he would grab the goods and run. After awhile, he would stick around to enjoy his treats. Another couple of weeks went by and he was waiting at the door for her. Then things progressed really rapidly. He was finally convinced that she was no threat and their friendship began. He was taking food right out of her and even letting her pet him.

Now the cat is completely adjusted, has free run of her entire house, and has met and made friends with the three other cats that live there. It's a very happy ending but the entire process took well over six months. This was an extreme case and the owner did everything right. Most people don't have this kind of patience and would have given the cat up as hopeless.

Most cats won't take this long to adjust, but they will adjust more quickly if you understand the cat and don't try to rush and force things.

How to Introduce a Cat to a New Home

Set the cat and all her needs up in one room. This gives her a small space to establish as her territory. If you set up too large a space for the cat, it will take longer for her to adjust.

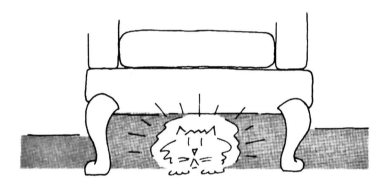

Ignore the cat and let her explore her new home in her own good time. Don't force or rush her.

Don't approach the cat. Let her come to you. You can try to speed this up by passively bribing her with treats. Don't offer the treats, just leave them lying out in clear view. If the cat doesn't come up to you, don't reach out to her, this may scare her off and the entire adjustment period will take longer. The treats are meant to speed up the cat approaching you, not you approaching the cat.

When the cat is obviously adjusted to you and her new room, then you can begin leaving the door to the rest of the house open. Again, don't force the cat out. Let her explore the rest of your house at her own pace. Usually the cat will venture out at night when you are asleep and you won't even know it. You can leave a few special treats just outside the doorway. If they are gone in the morning, then you know she at least ventured out that far. Every night you can leave the treats a little further from her room.

Simply allow the cat to come and go as she pleases. If something in the rest of the house scares her, she can always run back to the safety of home base to rebuild her courage before venturing forth again. Eventually she will adjust and be comfortable in your entire house.

Now you can move her litterbox and food bowls to an area that is more acceptable and convenient for you. But don't just one day have the litterbox disappear from its usual place and reappear somewhere else. Have two or three litterboxes and wait until the cat gets used to using them and knows exactly where they are before suddenly taking one away. It is better to have a litterbox in an inconvenient location and have the cat use it, than to have the cat eliminate on the carpet or in your closet.

Pack Your Bags Kitty, We're Moving to Kansas

If the cat already knows you and you are moving to a new house across town or to a different city, the adjustment process will be similar, but will progress much more quickly. The cat only has to get used to the new house since he already knows you. You can help your cat adjust by setting up his special room before bringing him in. Put lots of familiar items and furniture in the room. Things that have your scent and his on it are perfect as they will help him feel at home right away. Spend more time with him and reassure him constantly during the first month or so.

When owners move to a new home and let the cat outside right away, many of them are never seen again. It is just too much for the cat to cope with. Make sure your cat is fully adjusted to his indoor territory before forcing him to also adjust to his outside territory.

Before letting your cat outside on his own, let him observe the yard from the back porch. Put him on leash and take him for short jaunts in your yard interspersed with many retreats back to the house. It is essential that he becomes very familiar with how to get back to the house from all parts of his yard. When cats are startled or frightened, their tendency is to run to safety. You want to be sure he will run to your house, instead of out of the yard.

If your cat finds himself in unfamiliar territory, he will be lost, even if is just two houses away. Every owner should teach his cat the command, "Come here Kitty." If your cat will come when called, you can continually practice calling him to come in from outside to reinforce his escape route during his adjustment to his new outdoors. And, in case your cat is ever lost, it will be easier to find him if he knows to come when called.

Come Here Kitty

To train your cat to come when called is fairly easy. Most cats I know come running every time they hear the sound of an electric can opener. The sound tells them that dinner is about to be served. Instead of the can opener as the cue, you can use a verbal command or a sound such as a whistle.

Start the training when the cat is hungry. Get a few of his favorite treats and give him one for free to let him know a game is about to start. Hold out a second treat and back up about a yard, saying, "Come here kitty," and give him the treat when he comes. If he does not come, try using a more enticing treat or try again later when he has a better appetite. Most likely however, he will come running. Keep repeating this exercise, backing up farther and farther each time.

Practice in all the rooms of your house. Have two or more people go to different rooms in the house and call the cat back and forth. Practice calling him to come from just outside the doorway. Whenever he is outside, before he gets too far away, call him to come back. Give him a treat then let him go outside again.

Once he has the idea, there is no need to reward him each time. Most cats will respond more enthusiastically if rewarded once every five or six tries. The rule of thumb is: if the cat always comes, reward him less often. If the cat loses interest, reward him more often. Always reward the cat's speediest responses.

Personally, I think the best thing you can do for your cat as well as for yourself is to keep your cat indoors all the time. I guess this feeling comes from having seen too many stray, lost, injured and dead cats in both city and rural animal shelters. Letting cats roam outdoors is unfair and dangerous.

Outdoor cats are in constant danger from the hazards of modern living; they are more likely to get diseases and infections. They get into fights with other cats. Free roaming cats can be a nuisance to the neighborhood. Why should anyone have to put up with my cat using their garden as a litterbox? Why should they have to listen to incessant barking, when my cat teases dogs from rooftops and fences? I get just as many calls from people asking how to keep neighborhood cats out of their yards as I do from cat owners.

Many owners tell me they put the cat outside because the cat isn't litterbox trained, or because the cat is ruining their drapes. It would be much better for all concerned, especially the cat, if he was taught what was expected of him instead of being pushed out the front door. If your cat lives outside because he sprays, then read the chapter on litterbox problems and spraying. Your cat will be much happier indoors and so will you if kitty isn't spraying in your house.

If your cat is put outdoors because he claws your furniture, read the chapter on scratching furniture. Do not condemn your cat to an uncertain life or death outside. Cats live very happy and normal lives completely indoors if the time is taken to provide for their needs.

Some owners feel sorry for their cat when she meows loudly to go outside. That's because they are not there to see her and feel sorry for her when she's hiding under a car or up a tree because she's being terrorized by a dog, kids, or another cat.

If the cat doesn't know enough to stay off furniture, how in the world is she going to know to stay off the streets. If our toddler screams to play in the street, we don't let him. If your pre-teenage child whines that she wants to go to an all night drinking party just because her friends are going, you don't feel sorry for her and say OK.

If you want to provide your cat some fresh air and natural light, provide an open screened window or an outdoor wire enclosure attached to a window. Teach your cat to walk on a leash and take her for walks, even if it's just in your own back yard. If you think your cat may be lonely, a second cat for companionship may be helpful.

What? You're Bringing Home Another Cat?

When selecting a new cat, try to find one that has previously lived with other cats. It is best to introduce a cat that is different in age and sex to the resident cat. Fighting usually occurs between cats of the same sex and age, especially between toms.

When you bring the cat home, follow the same steps outlined earlier about bringing in a new cat. While the cat is adjusting to you and her new territory, you should be spending time and energy with your resident cats. They are the ones who are going to feel that their territory is being invaded and may react by marking, acting aggressive or being destructive. Some cats get so upset that they pack their bags and leave and may never come back.

It is especially important to prepare your cats for the arrival of a newcomer. Spend lots of time concentrating on rewarding and praising their good behavior. Most likely they will react by not using their litterbox. So even if the litterbox is not a problem now, it's a good idea to read the chapter on litterbox problems to help avoid this problem from occurring.

Most owners make such a big fuss over the newcomer, that the resident cat feels neglected, ignored and jealous. You should be doing just the opposite. Most of your attention should be given to the cats who have been with you the longest. Make absolutely sure that they feel secure with you and in their home territory before, during and after the newcomer's arrival.

When the new cat seems to be adjusting to you and his new room, you can start to familiarize the cats with each other. Start off by letting them get used to the smell of each other. Bring a piece of the resident cat's bedding into the new cat's room. Take some of his bedding and put it where your other cats can smell it. Keep exchanging and rotating their beds or a towel that covers their favorite sleeping area. Let the cats sniff each other from under the door or through a carrier/crate.

Once the new cat is adjusted to you and his own territory and all the cats have had plenty of opportunity to adjust to each other's scent and none of the cats act like they want to break the door down to kill the other, then it is time to begin leaving the door open.

The new cat will eventually creep out and meet the resident cat. What usually happens is that they both freeze, arch their backs, hiss, spit and even growl at each other. Then they both flee to safety. Should they have any squabbles, the newcomer can retreat to his own room. The resident cat will be less likely to enter because the room bears the scent of the newcomer.

The security and familiarity of the newcomer's own room will help rebuild his confidence to venture forth again. Most of their first encounters will appear hostile to you, but it is best not to interfere. Let them work things out by themselves. They will understand and get to know each other much quicker if you are not there to confuse the issues. If the cats are really aggressive towards each other and simply cannot adjust, read the section on fighting.

3

Beyond The Sandbox

The most common problem cat owners experience with their cats has to do with the litterbox. In fact, over 75% of my cat-owner clients call me because of litterbox problems. If you don't have a litterbox problem now, let me congratulate you for not skipping this chapter! Owners never call me until they already have a big problem. It is far easier to prevent this problem than it is to cure it. If you take active steps now, you can prevent a future problem. If not, your number will eventually come up; your cat will stop using the litterbox; and you will become part of the 75% statistic!

Don't Hold Your Breath

Let's look at the litterbox itself. The single most common reason a cat will refuse to use his box is because the box is dirty - from the cat's point of view. Cats have an extremely keen sense of smell and although the box might appear clean to you, it doesn't to the cat. Have you ever stopped at a gas station restroom? You take one step into the bathroom, immediately hold your nose, and think about going in the bushes along side the road. You would like to use the facilities provided, but they are so obnoxious and unpleasant, you're almost forced to go somewhere else.

Most owners I consult with say they change the litterbox on average, once a week. How would you like to use your own bathroom if you only flushed the toilet once a week?

B 12, G 47... Bingo !

A lot of owners tell me that their cat misses the litterbox. The first time I heard this I didn't know what they were talking about. Further questioning revealed that the cat eliminates two inches outside the box. Getting a larger litterbox did not solve the problem. You've all seen a cat defecate. The cat digs a little hole about the size of a quarter, he shifts this way and he shifts that way, and carefully positions himself. Then Bingo! It's a bulls-eye every time. Cats don't miss. If the feces is not in the box, the cat did not intend for it to go in the box. The cat is trying to tell you that he would like to use the box, but he's repelled by the smell and wetness.

A Cause to Refresh

The single most important thing you can do with the litterbox is to keep it clean. Simply scooping it out once a day is not enough. It is better to use less litter and dump it all out every day. Wash out the litterbox then rinse it with a diluted lemon juice or vinegar solution to help cut the ammonia smell.

I went into a grocery store one day and could not believe my eyes! I picked up a package of cat litter and the instructions printed on the side of the package said to clean the litterbox with ammonia. Do not use ammonia based products to clean the litterbox, it smells like stale, old urine to the cat.

The More the Merrier

Something else to consider is whether or not you have the right number of litterboxes. I usually recommend one box per cat plus one. So if you have one cat, you should have two boxes; and if you have two cats, you should have three boxes. Some cats can be extremely territorial about their box. They may refuse to use one of the boxes simply because another cat in the house used it. Occasionally the dominant cat in the household will protect the box from the other cat.

An especially fearful cat may be afraid to approach the box. There may be something between himself and the litterbox that he is afraid of. Suppose the cat is in the bedroom when the urge overcomes him. He pokes his head out of the room and sees you getting out the vacuum cleaner. You and the vacuum are between kitty and the litterbox. Instead of having to pass by the vacuum, the cat will eliminate somewhere else. But if there was a second litterbox, there wouldn't be a problem.

Having more than one box also increases the chances that one of them will be clean enough for the cat's satisfaction. And you know how cats are, their definition of clean and dirty changes every day.

Litterbox, Litterbox, Where Are You ?

There are a few other things to keep in mind about the litterbox. Is it located in the right area? Cats do not like to have their litterbox too close to their food and bedding. They do like to have a consistent and private place to do their business. So don't put the box in the busiest room of your house.

Occasionally there may be something about the box or location of the box that inhibits the cat from using it. I remember one woman who accidentally dropped a roll of toilet paper on the cat's head while he was in the box. Another person turned on the shower before closing the curtain and the cat got sprayed with water while in the litterbox. Both of these cats were afraid to even go into the bathroom, much less use the litterbox there after these experiences. We had to temporarily put the boxes just outside the bathroom door.

It may seem like common sense, but is the box easy for the cat to get to? I'm surprised at how many owners keep the box in a closet and then forget to leave the closet door open!

Another owner kept moving the box every day trying to find a place where his dog could not get into it. The dog didn't have trouble finding it, but the cat sure wasn't very happy about the situation.

And what about the litter itself? Every cat has his own likes and dislikes, but most cats like clean, absorbent litter that feels and smells natural to them. Sometimes they are repelled by fancy litters with all sorts of additives and perfumes that are more for our benefit than for the cats.

I've Cleaned Up the Act, But . . .

OK, so you have a clean litterbox with the right litter and it's located in a quiet, private, easy-to-get-to place. Now what? Many cats won't magically start using their box again just because you've started keeping it clean.

First of all, the cat won't know that the box is really clean. After all, it's been dirty for the last six months so why should things be any different now? He will just assume it's still dirty and go straight to where he knows it will be clean. Whenever the cat pees in the closet or poops under the piano, you don't let it sit there for a week. You clean it up immediately! The cat keeps going back there because he knows it's always clean.

I drive from San Francisco to Los Angeles and there are a few gas stations along the way that I simply don't stop at anymore because I've learned from experience that their facilities are never clean. I'm not going to waste my time stopping to check them out, even if they posted a sign that read, "Attention! Our bathrooms have been cleaned!" I would just laugh and drive right on by. So your cat too probably looks at the litterbox, laughs and cruises right on by.

Some owners go berserk when they find puddles or piles somewhere in the house. Often times they scream, grab the cat and throw her in the litterbox - or they grab the cat's paws and force her to dig in the litter. Cats hate to be forced into doing anything. These cats avoid the box because they have learned that it's a torture chamber. They associate the box with unpleasant experiences.

In order to turn this all around, you must convince the cat that the litterbox is both a clean and pleasant place to be. Whenever your cat is hungry or in a playful mood, get out a special treat or her favorite toy and lure her near her box.

If those gas stations had a sign that read, "Ten dollars to everyone who checks out our facilities," you bet I wouldn't just drive by and laugh. These guys are actively trying to convince me that they've changed their ways and their human litterboxes are clean and pleasant. You can apply the same bribery techniques and principles to your cat.

Most hungry cats will happily follow a chunk of turkey dangling in front of his nose. Entice kitty to follow the tasty treat or a toy to his box, then enthusiastically praise and reward kitty when you get to the box. Within a short time, kitty will get the hang of the game and you can begin calling him to come towards you and the box from different locations in your home.

Work especially hard to call kitty away from areas he has soiled in the past. When he arrives at the box, profusely praise and reward him. Now kitty will see that not only is the box clean, but it's also a rewarding and pleasant place to be. The next step is to praise and reward him for times he actually uses his box.

What Goes In, Must Come Out

We expect cats to train themselves because cats are instinctively clean. Litterbox training will progress much more quickly if you can reward and praise your cat when he is using his box. The timing of the reward is extremely important. In order to effectively reward kitty for using the box, you must be there when he uses it.

If you must be there to reward him, then obviously you need to know when he has to go, or you'll be hanging around the litterbox forever. This brings up the importance of schedules. A cat's physical system is like clock work. If the input is at the same time every day, the output will take on a corresponding schedule. Once you know the approximate time your cat will need to eliminate, you can arrange to be present to reward and praise him when he eliminates in the box.

Now you only have to hang around the box for about 15 minutes instead of all day long. If you keep an eye on your cat during this time, you can also prevent him from going near those places that he used to soil.

If It's Still Not Working

For severe litterbox problems, it may be necessary to confine your cat with a litterbox, her toys, scratching post and bed to one room for a few days. By confining your cat, she can more quickly learn to use her box. First, if you and your cat are both in the same room, then it will be easier for you to keep an eye on her, so it will be easier for you to praise and reward her at the exact right moment.

Second, if you're not there, the chances are higher that she will use the box on her own. If given the choice of using litter or a linoleum or tile floor, your cat will choose the litter which absorbs the urine and gives her the opportunity and ability to cover her feces.

Cats are creatures of habit. They usually return to

the same places to their business. So additionally, confinement is used to help break the cat's habit of eliminating in inappropriate areas. If she doesn't have access to these areas, then she doesn't have the opportunity to keep reinforcing her old habit.

If you are turned off to the idea of confinement, then you probably don't really understand it. Maybe you've tried it in the past, went about it the wrong way and had a bad experience, or the cat had a bad experience. If your attitude is that confinement is a prison sentence, then it is not going to work. Confinement should be a positive and rewarding training experience. Review the section that explains the use and purposes of temporary confinement.

Summary

1. The litterbox must always be clean. Sometimes all it can take is neglecting the box just once and the cat will feel forced to go somewhere else. Now you have to start all over again retraining your cat to use his box. So don't forget to clean the box without fail.

2. Make sure you have the right number of litterboxes in appropriate locations with the right litter.

3. Praise and reward your cat whenever you see her use her box. During initial training, it is important to be present as much as possible to reward your cat

when she uses the box. Once your cat is trained, it is still equally as important to maintain the training by regularly praising your cat anytime you see her use the box. If you forget to reward your cat, she may forget to use her box. Never take good behavior for granted or you may find yourself having to retrain your cat to use her box.

4. Training may require the use of confinement. This is only a temporary measure to speed up the training process and to help break bad habits.

Great Scott !! He Must Be Spraying

Litterbox training takes care of your cat's physiological need to eliminate. However, cats will also leave their urine and feces in inappropriate places as a form of marking. This is a social, sexual and territorial behavior.

The classic or most common marking behavior is urine-spraying by unneutered male cats. But both male and female, neutered and intact will mark. They can mark with feces as well as urine and the urine can be either sprayed or left in puddles.

In Chapter 2, we looked at the cat's strong territorial nature. If you haven't read that chapter, it will be useful in helping you understand your cat's need to identify his territory through scent.

Any intrusion on the cat's territory, whether human, animal or even a new piece of furniture, can cause a cat to feel threatened, insecure and stressed. This results in his need to remind the world and himself of his territory. A confident, secure, contented and relaxed cat does not need to relieve anxiety and stress by such extreme measures as urine marking. Almost anything can upset the delicate sensitivity of the cat. Too many cats in the house, a new cat or dog in the neighborhood, a visitor from out of town, a family member away on vacation, any change in routine or change in environment can cause stress in the cat's life causing him to begin marking or stop using his litterbox.

Several studies have shown that outdoor cats cover their feces on their home territory but not at their territory's edge. This could be a form of marking behavior. So if your cat suddenly starts defecating all over the house or in certain rooms, he may be telling you that he is feeling threatened or insecure.

The most common offenders are unneutered male cats and the simplest cure is to have the cat neutered. But even neutered male cats will sometimes spray. In this case, hormones, pheromones, pharmaceuticals and alternative therapies have been used very successfully in stopping the problem.

However, you should discuss this thoroughly with your veterinarian. There are different kinds of therapies, different dosages and different lengths of treatment. As with many medications, there can be side effects.

Neutering and hormonal treatment take time to take effect. You may need to change the type or dosage of hormone if you don't see results. Too many owners think that neutering, a shot or a pill will magically stop the marking behavior overnight. It can actually take several weeks before there is any behavioral change.

So have patience and keep in touch with your veterinarian.

It is also usually not necessary to treat the cat for very long. Sometimes an active, adolescent male will only need a seasonal shot so he isn't frustrated by the neighborhood female cats in heat. Maybe the cat needs one shot just to get him through a particularly stressful time in his life, like when you move into a hew home. Once he has adjusted, the need to mark will disappear.

Some veterinarians recommend tranquilizers and anti-anxiety drugs for treatment of marking behavior as well as other behavior problems. This makes sense because they calm the cat and reduce stress. I personally feel that the tranquilizer should be given to the owner as well as the cat. If the owner could just relax and calm down, perhaps the cat's life wouldn't be so stressful.

Recently, I received several anxious messages from a very distressed sounding woman. She spoke so fast I could barely understand her, but I think she said her cat was peeing on her bed. In the first message, she did not leave her phone number. A week later, her second message didn't leave her name but I recognized her voice, but still no phone number. Eventually she frantically told me to please call her as soon as possible but she could only be reached at her number on Tuesdays from 8:00 to 8:15; on Wednesdays from 10:45 to 11:15; and on every other

Friday from 6:00 to 6:20. The message had an assortment of days and times but I didn't know if these were morning or evening times. Needless to say, I never did reach her at any of those times, but I did give it my best shot. What annoyed me even further was that she didn't have an answering machine. No wonder she was having problems with her cat!

Some marking behavior is actually caused by the owners themselves. They don't understand their cat's behavior and consequently resort to the most absurd and cruel forms of punishment. These outbursts of anger and misuse of punishment stresses the cat out so much that it causes the cat to spray even more.

I had one case where the owner would come home from work and march straight to his stereo speakers. If he saw one new claw mark, he would grab his cat, throw her into the shower and turn the water on. It wasn't long before the cat began urinating all over his house. Once he understood his cat, stopped the punishment and taught her to use a scratching post, both the stereo scratching and urine marking stopped.

Instead of using drugs, I think you can accomplish the same thing through the use of the holistic therapy I discussed in chapter one. Basically, it's sharing quality time with your cat. Help your cat feel happy, secure, relaxed and confident in his own home and territory. Play games with him, give him a massage, talk to him , but give him some very positive and affectionate attention. You know what your cat likes - just do it. This does a lot more to reduce stress and anxiety than the use of drugs. Proper diet and exercise are also important in maintaining a happy, healthy cat.

Some people recommend placing aluminum foil or the cat's food bowls in areas where the cat sprays. The cat is supposed to be repelled by the noise and splashing of the urine on the foil, and they also don't like to soil their eating area. Sometimes this works, and it's easy enough to give it a try, but often the cat will just spray somewhere else. One frustrated cat owner finally called me for help when she realized that half her home was covered in foil and she had 17 food bowls on the floor in various locations. Even if this method works, it is usually only temporary because it doesn't get to the root of the problem which is the cat's mental and emotional well-being.

Summary

Territorial marking is an expression of your cat's psychological state. The combination of neutering, positive reward training and stress reduction are the keys to solving this problem.

Doctor ! Doctor !

Sometimes a cat will go off her litterbox for medical reasons. It is always a good idea to have your cat checked by your veterinarian anytime you notice a change in behavior or any unusual behavior. Cats are prone to urinary tract problems. If your cat urinates in small puddles, if you see blood in the urine or if your cat urinates on cool ceramic surfaces, such as sinks, bathtubs or stove tops, these are common signs that the cat is having a medical problem that needs immediate veterinary attention.

If a litterbox problem is caused by illness or infection, your cat will not necessarily return to using the box when the condition is cured. A habit of eliminating somewhere other than in the litterbox may already be strongly established. Your cat may associate the litterbox with pain and discomfort. So once your cat is cured, you might need to do some standard praise and reward litterbox training as outlined in the first part of this chapter.

Warning ! Danger ! Alert !

One more reminder: Never punish your cat for not using the litterbox, even if you catch him in the act. Any punishment can cause the cat to feel threatened, insecure and stressed - and these things only make the problem worse.

He might learn to be afraid of eliminating in front of you. So you won't have the opportunity to reward or praise him for using the litterbox.

Remember Robert the ballet cat from Chapter 1? Cats learn best by your rewarding and praising their good behavior.

4

The Last Claw

Cats enjoy clawing, scratching and climbing. They need to scratch. It conditions their nails, allows them to stretch and exercise their paw muscles and it also marks their territory. Cats have scent glands in their feet and when they scratch, they leave behind not only a visual mark, but a scent mark too.

Outdoor cats have favorite scratching sites; usually it's one particular tree and the cat keeps returning to it, both out of habit and to freshen up the scent already placed on the tree. Indoor cats develop a favorite scratching area too. Unfortunately, this favorite spot may be your stereo speakers, furniture or drapes.

The first step is to take advantage of your cat's preferred location for scratching. Let's say it's your couch. Temporarily move it to a different spot. Moving it just a few feet is enough. Then place a scratching post exactly where the part of the couch was that the cat was clawing. Once the scratching post is in place, you must teach your cat to use her post.

At the same time, make the couch an undesirable place to scratch. Cover the part of the couch that kitty likes with something she does not like. Cats usually don't like the feel of aluminum foil. They also don't like to snag their claws when scratching, so you can cover the couch with something like cheesecloth. You can put an unpleasant scent on a towel and drape that over the couch. Many cats are repelled by the scent of citrus or menthol. Whatever you cat does not like, that's what you should use. Your pet store should carry products designed specifically to repel or discourage contact. You know your cat best, sometimes something as simple as 2-sided tape will do the job.

The Sky Is Falling

Most cats respond well to booby traps. To make a simple booby trap, take several empty soda cans and put a few pennies in them. If you were to shake one of these cans or if it were to fall on the floor, it would make a horrible racket and startle the cat. Tie a piece of string to a few of these cans and then tack the string across the area that kitty usually scratches. When kitty's claw pulls the string, all the cans come crashing down and kitty will flee to safety. Most cats will never approach or try to scratch that item again. But reset the booby trap anyway and leave it there until you are sure the cat won't return to try it again. Some cats just can't believe what happened and will some back for a second lesson.

Remember, while you are discouraging kitty from scratching an undesired area, you need to teach her to use her post for all her scratching needs. It is rare for a cat to just automatically start clawing a post. You must take the time to teach her to use it.

April Fools !

First of all, don't force kitty to use her post. Some people grab the cat's paws and force them to scratch. Cats do not like being forced into doing anything. They will just resist and resent you. Instead, you have to lure and trick kitty into thinking that she has discovered this new and exciting thing all by herself.

Take one of her favorite toys and drag it around on the end of a piece of string. Slowly and gradually pull the toy near the post. When kitty is really into the game and having fun, drag the toy up the post. As she swats and pounces on it, her paws and claws will eventually find that the post is a fun thing to scratch on. Give hers lots of praise, rewards and encouragement for playing with her toys around the post. It is a good idea to get a post with ledges built into it so that she can climb up and sit on it too.

If your cat likes catnip, rub some on her scratching post to entice her into approaching it. Try placing special treats and goodies on different levels of the post so she gets even more rewards for visiting and climbing there.

The Invisible Cat

Until your cat has learned to use her post, try to make life itself revolve around it. The post should be the center of her universe. Feed her there, talk to her and play with her there. Withhold any and all affection and attention unless she is by her post. Soon she will learn that the post is a good luck charm and all kinds of wonderful things happen near it.

To make this method work, it is essential that you ignore her at all other times. Just pretend she is not there. She is invisible unless she is at her post. If she comes to you for attention, then go sit by her post before giving any attention. Anytime you see her near the post and especially if she is using it, make a big fuss over her. Let her know how happy you are and that special things happen whenever she is at her scratching post. Before you know it, she will always be hanging around her post.

Now you can up the ante. In order for the charm (scratching post) to work, she must now be scratching or climbing it. Start ignoring her when she is at the post; especially now because she will always be there. Wait until she scratches or climbs it, and then flood her with affection, attention and treats.

When you are sure she has developed a habit of using her post, you can start to slowly move it to a location that is more desirable and convenient for you. Move it so slowly that she doesn't realize what is happening. By slowly, I mean about an inch or less every few days. It won't take that long and it is certainly better to move it too slowly than to have her stop using it. Once it is gradually moved to a different place, then you can move the couch back to its original location.

Even when the problem is solved, never take good behavior for granted. Always let kitty know how pleased you are and how good she is when she scratches her post. Continue to give her special attention and treats for scratching it, never ignore her during those times or she may start doing other things to get your attention.

If you see kitty trying to claw something other than her post, it is better for you not to say anything to her. She may learn to get your attention by doing this or she may start doing it when you are not looking.

It is much better to just suddenly make a loud noise or toss a magazine in her direction to startle her out of the behavior. Wait a little while and then call her over to her post and play with her there. Do not give her the opportunity to develop a habit of scratching anything other than her post. If you see her tempted to scratch on something else, immediately booby trap it or cover it.

Every time she claws on something and it's a pleasant experience, the more likely she will return to scratch it again. The more she scratches it, the more the habit is being established. Don't delay and say you will do it tomorrow. Do it today. The longer you wait, the more difficult it will be break the habit. It is also a good idea to go back to the routine of withholding treats, affection and attention unless she is at her post - and there, it is heaven on earth for her.

But My Living Room is
One Giant Scratching Post !

If your cat has an extremely bad case of destructive behavior and is scratching everything in sight, then it is best to set up a playroom for him with several scratching posts. He will develop a habit of using the posts because there simply isn't anything else in his playroom to scratch. The habit of scratching the furniture will also be broken because he doesn't have access to it. Review the section on confinement from Chapter 1.

When your cat has firmly established the habit of scratching on his various posts, then you can bring him out with all the posts. Make sure you do this when you know you have lots of time and energy to devote to him. You are going to have to temporarily rearrange your household furniture, but it will be worth it.

Take the items he used to scratch on, move them and booby trap them. Then put his posts at those locations. He should be attracted to the posts because they now have his scent on them. Make sure everyone in the household understands that all food, treats, play and affection are withheld unless he is at or near one of his posts. Within a short time, you can start slowly moving the posts to more convenient locations and moving your furniture back.

Summary

1. Provide and teach kitty to use a scratching post through the use of praise and reward.

2. Make the items you don't want her to claw unattractive by booby trapping them. If you see her scratching a forbidden item, make a loud, startling noise.

3. Do not punish kitty when he misbehaves. This will cause him to misbehave to get your attention or he will never scratch anything in front of you. If he will never scratch in front of you, then you will not be able to reward him for scratching appropriately. You will also not be able to make a loud noise when he scratches inappropriate items because you will never see him do it. Punishment almost always makes the problem worse or creates other problems such as urine marking. Review the dangers of using punishment from the first chapter.

5

Toxic Taste

What about cats that eat plants? There are several theories as to why they do it. It could be a nutritional deficiency; it could be that it helps the cat regurgitate when his stomach is upset or he has hairballs; or it could be that he has intestinal parasites. So the very first thing you should do is have kitty get a clean bill of health from your veterinarian.

However, most cats that eat plants are quite healthy and do it out of fun or habit. In any case, it is a dangerous habit and should be stopped immediately. Many household and garden plants are poisonous to cats. The most important thing you can do is to find out if the plants you have are OK. Get rid of any plants that you know can be harmful and all plants that are questionable.

This may seem extreme, but there are so many plants available for your enjoyment, why take a chance? It is much better and safer to have non-toxic ones in your home. Check with your veterinarian or the internet for a list of plants that are toxic to cats.

Even after you have trained your cat to leave your plants alone, no one, including your cat, is perfect. If kitty forgets or makes just one mistake, it could cost you her life. Until you have the time to investigate which plants are safe, don't give your cat access to them. It's just not worth it. Either confine your cat to a room that doesn't have any plants, or put all the plants in one room and shut the door.

If your cat likes to eat plants, let's not deny her that simple enjoyment. Instead, here are two things you can do.

Eat Your Vegetables

First, provide her with her own kitty garden. Many pet stores sell seeds and live greens you can grow yourself for her pleasure. Teach her that this is her special garden and she can dine there anytime she desires. You may have to encourage her at first by making her special greens really enticing and attractive. Try smearing some tuna oil or salmon on some of the leaves. That should do the trick. Praise and reward her for eating at her own salad bar.

Don't Eat The Daisies

Second, once she has learned to use her own garden regularly, it is time to teach her to leave your plants alone. Introduce your plants back into your home, but as something your cat will want to avoid.

Start with one luxurious sample that is edible. Paint the underside of the leaves with a very hot pepper oil, lemon or peppermint oil. Most cats I know don't like these, but if your cat does, then you need to find something your cat really dislikes. Spray the top of the leaves with a diluted perfume. A 1:100 dilution with water will do. You don't want your entire house to reek of perfume. You only want your cat with his keen sense of smell to detect it.

Place the plant in the middle of your living room floor and let your cat investigate. Make the plant more irresistible by tying a piece of string to a couple of the leaves and tugging from a distance. This will entice your cat to approach and hopefully take a bite. When he does, he will learn that this plant tastes awful! Kitty should now associate the scent with the horrible taste in his mouth and will not want to taste anything that smells like that again.

Over the next week, move the booby trapped plant to different locations in your house. Regularly spruce up the taste deterrent and perfume. Try this same procedure with another plant to be sure kitty gets the message. If he does, spray all your other plants with the diluted perfume and bring them back into your house. Regularly spray all your plants with the solution to remind him to stay away from them.

If kitty is climbing into the potted plants to use them as a litterbox, then you have a different problem. Try putting aluminum foil or small ragged rocks over the dirt to discourage her and at the same time refer to the chapter on litterbox problems.

Summary

1. Don't have plants in your home or garden that could possibly threaten the health of your cat.

2. Provide kitty with her own garden and teach her to eat there through the use of reward and praise.

3. Discourage your cat from eating your houseplants by making them unpleasant and unrewarding. Let the plant itself say, "Stay away," rather than you telling her. If you reprimand her, she will just learn to eat the plants when you aren't watching or she will do it just to get your attention. Punishment by you only makes things worse.

4. Continue to spruce up the booby traps on the forbidden plants and spruce up your rewards for her eating from her own garden.

6

Driving Miss Crazy

Most cats are not hyperactive. They just have a lot of energy to burn. What you might think is hyperactivity is usually normal cat behavior but it's driving you crazy! And when your cat goes bonkers at three in the morning, the sleep deprivation it causes can drive you insane!

Cats are nocturnal and it is normal for them to be active at night. If they had their choice, they would sleep all day and do all their cat things at night and early in the morning. If your cat's nocturnal activities bother you, be sure you aren't accidentally training and rewarding kitty for her behavior.

When kitty pounces on your face at 4:00 AM, don't get up and feed her or play with her or your cat will come to expect it. She will try to wake you up every morning for her pre-breakfast snack or play session. Instead of losing your patience, change your cat's schedule to coincide with your own. Instead of letting her sleep all day, play with her and exercise her during the day, especially in the evening and just before your own bedtime.

Make sure your cat is so played-out and tired that she will sleep all night long. It will take awhile for your cat to adjust and she will probably still wake up early out of habit for a few days. But eventually she will sleep in later and later.

When she does wake you up too early, make it absolutely clear that the consequences are definitely unpleasant. Don't leave any room for misinterpretation or misunderstanding. Either spray kitty in the face with water, burst a balloon or point your hair dryer at her and blast away. Whatever you do, the cat must realize without a doubt that the consequences of trying to wake you up are negative. It may sound like a lot of work to keep a plant sprayer or hair dryer within easy reach at 4 in the morning, but the results will be worth it.

This unpleasant counter attack on your cat will only work if you are at the same time providing him with daytime and late night activities. If you expect your cat to stay awake all day long, forget it, he won't. Cats are naturally nocturnal. If your only action is reprimand, you will make the problem worse and create other behavior problems.

For Crying Out Loud !

If your cat meows excessively, it is most likely because you have inadvertently trained him to meow. Your cat has learned to meow to get whatever he wants - food, attention or affection. Often, what starts out as a demand for attention becomes a self-reinforcing habit. Now kitty will meow all day just for the fun of it. The situation becomes even worse if your cat is lonely or bored.

Pay attention to kitty and give him whatever he wants, but only when he is quiet. Ignore him whenever he begins his vocal blackmail. Don't give in. Each time you give in to your cat's verbal demands, you are teaching him to meow even more. If you wait until your cat is quiet, he will soon learn to associate silence with rewards. This is often difficult to remember because the meowing gets our attention. It's easy to overlook and ignore kitty when he is quiet.

I arrived at one client's home and found a huge sign on the door that said, "Please knock quietly!" The owner greeted me with whispers and instructed me not to make any noise. When I asked why we had to be so quiet, she replied that we might disturb her cat. As soon as anyone paid any attention to him, he would not be quiet until they left. This cat had associated all human interaction with meowing. If he even saw you looking at him, he would start up.

Some cats enjoy "talking," and some owners enjoy their cat's chatting to them. But if you want a few moments of peace, you can teach your cat to be quiet on request. Gently ask kitty to "Shush." If your cat ignores you, immediately shout, "BE QUIET!" or squirt him in the face with water.

After a few repetitions, kitty will get the idea and obey the gentle request of "Shush," rather than get screamed at or doused with water. Be sure to always give him the request first. It isn't fair to reprimand his meowing without first letting him know that you've had enough. We don't want him to think that you get obnoxious without reason or warning. If he does obey your request, don't forget to tell him what a good boy he is!

Are We Having an Earthquake ?

Sometimes cats go into a wild frenzy of activity. They will climb the walls, bounce off furniture, chase phantom spirits and practically destroy the house in the process. Cats have energy and need to release it. It is much better to help your cat vent his energy in a controlled setting rather than letting him go bonkers whenever he feels the need. Set aside some time and schedule your cat's play sessions. That way you will be present to supervise.

Give him fun and active things to do. Teaching a few simple tricks can be a fun and rewarding way for both you and your cat to play together. It is also an excellent way to give your cat a good, physical workout.

Teach your cat to play fetch. Attach a line to the end of a toy, throw it down the hallway and reel it back in. Don't just give your cat a few toys and expect her to know what to do with them. She can't read the package label that says, "cat toy." You have to get on the floor with your cat and show her how to play with her toys.

Take out a few of your cat's favorite treats. Have him run back and forth between you and another person to get his reward. It's even more fun with three people. Call out kitty's name, wave the treat in front of his nose, then back up. If he follows, give him the treat when you get across the room. After a few times, all you have to do is call his name and he should come running to get his reward. Try enticing him to follow you by waving his favorite catnip mouse in front of him.

Tie a feather or piece of crumpled paper to the end of a length of string and trail it around the house with kitty in hot pursuit. There are dozens of cat toys and ideas for home-made toys at your pet store.

Get a hoop and teach kitty to jump through it. Start out by holding the hoop between your cat and a tasty treat. Your cat will have to step over the bottom of the hoop to get to the treat. Slowly and gradually raise the hoop up off the floor so that he has to step up higher and higher to get across. Eventually he will have to jump through it in order to get his reward. Even if things don't go that well, so what? You're not trying out for a Walt Disney production.

What you are doing is spending time with your cat and having fun. Don't take it too seriously. If it isn't fun for your cat, he won't want to play. Remember, the idea here is to have constructive play sessions with your cat while you are present to control and monitor him. A tired, happy cat won't have the excess energy to go crazy and cause trouble when you're trying to sleep or when you are not home.

If you want kitty to really sleep in in the morning, then it's best to play these games as late as possible before going to bed.

Summary

1. Cats are nocturnal. If you don't like the night shift, it's up to you to modify their natural schedule.

2. Don't inadvertently reward your cat for waking you up. Feeding him, playing with him or giving him any kind of attention at all will be interpreted as a reward.

3. Provide your cat with regular, constructive and active play time. Don't expect him to play by himself.

Regardless of what your cat is doing, whether he's clawing your favorite chair, attacking your plants, waking you up at 3 AM, or using your bed for his litterbox - your cat is acting in a way he thinks appropriate. He isn't personally trying to get back at you for anything. He may be doing it to get your attention or you may have inadvertently rewarded and trained him to do these things.

Don't punish kitty for being a cat. Instead, teach him the rules of your home - but teach him in a way he can understand. Your cat will be much happier and so will you.

7

Soothing The Savage Beast

Most of us tend to look on our cats as cute, warm, furry, harmless pets. We forget that they are animals and can be potentially dangerous. There are trainers who can put their heads into the mouths of lions, yet we have little kittycats that bite and scratch us. If kitty was a lion cub, we would probably do something right away to be sure she learned never to hurt us.

Cats as a whole are domesticated, but each and every cat must be handled and gentled individually and taught not to scratch and bite people.

It's rare that cats bite or scratch because they're just plain mean and nasty. There are two common reasons why they may "attack" you. The first is out of play and fun. Cats are predators by nature and the games they play are an extension of this trait. Since cats don't have to go out and catch dinner everyday, they still have this energy to vent and need to practice up on their hunting skills. This is normal cat behavior.

When cats stalk prey, they often lie in wait for what seems to be an eternity; staring, sometimes creeping. Suddenly there's a burst of energy and the cat pounces on its victim. Often, the victim is the owner. Cats love to attack human feet in play and love to pounce on waving arms, wiggling fingers, or just about anything that moves.

By reacting to this play in the wrong way, we unintentionally reinforce the behavior. The cat thinks we enjoy these games and so continues to play them.

Friday the 13th

Your cat may feel loving and affectionate one moment and jump in your lap hoping to be stroked. After awhile, he's had enough. But he can't verbally say to you, "Uh, excuse me but I think I've had enough." Instead he tells you in the only way he knows how - by biting or scratching. When the cat swats at us, we do exactly what he wants. We stop petting him. This only compounds the problem and reinforces the behavior.

Your cat may give you a gentle nibble that you interpret as a love bite. Since we know that the cat doesn't mean any harm, we often excuse it and let the cat get away with it. I've seen many owners giggle and give their cat a kiss in return. Now kitty thinks we like to be bitten. It is very confusing to the cat when one minute we reward biting and next reprimand it.

Other reasons a cat will bite or scratch is because he is frightened, angry, hurt or feeling threatened. If the cat doesn't want to be picked up, put in a box and hauled off to the vet, he will often resist by biting and scratching. Again, we compound this problem by doing one of two things. Either we leave the cat alone so he learns to get his way and control us by acting defensive; or we continue to force kitty into doing something he doesn't want to do, causing him to feel even more threatened, frightened and defensive.

So What Do We Do ?

First, if your cat is biting and scratching you in play, let's see how we can communicate our displeasure in a way the cat can understand.

When kittens and cats play together, they learn to play gently. They pounce and tumble, bite without any pressure and swat at each other just with their paws, not with their claws. If one cat accidentally gets a little too rough and hurts the other, the one that is hurt instantly hisses and runs away. The offending kitty is suddenly left with no one to play with. It doesn't take too many repetitions for the cat to learn that if she wants to continue to play, she must be gentler.

You can do exactly the same thing. Whenever kitty starts to bite or her claws come out, you simply screech, hiss and walk away. By doing this, you are telling your cat that if she isn't going to play nicely, then you are not going to play at all. If she immediately comes running back to play some more, just ignore her. This isolation is a powerful way to communicate with your cat.

Don't wait until you're bleeding before you stop the play session. As soon as you think she looks like she's getting too rough or as soon as her claws come out, but before she actually scratches you, stop playing. If she puts her claws away or starts to calm down, then resume playing, otherwise get up and walk away. With this method, kitty will learn to not even think about biting or scratching you, and you won't have to endure a lot of scratches and bites while she is learning.

At the same time, realize that your cat has certain needs. She needs to be able to play out her predatory instincts. So while she is learning not to use you for this purpose, you should also provide her with toys and games where she can release this energy. Tie a toy to the end of a piece of string and trail it around the house for her. Let her pounce on and attack it instead of you.

Schedule regular play sessions with her, so she won't have the need or energy to play at inappropriate times. For more ideas on how to help your cat release her energy, so she isn't as likely to release it on you or your household, review the chapter on hyperactive behavior.

I Like A Slow Hand

If your cat is biting and clawing because he is frightened or feeling threatened, then you must help your cat overcome his fears. A confident and secure cat doesn't feel the need to defend himself by acting aggressive.

Many cats don't like being picked up, hugged, having their tails and ears tugged, mouth looked into or paws held. This is normal cat behavior. I don't know any child who enjoys having his ears cleaned by his mother. And I don't know any adult who loves to go to the dentist. You never see the headlines of your local newspaper say, "Dentist mauled by patient getting his teeth cleaned." But we have cats that try to maul the veterinarian as well as their owners. You can't expect cats to just naturally accept these things. We have to show them and teach them.

We can't verbally try to explain to our cat that we're not going to hurt him when we pick him up or hold his paw to take a close look at it. Cats learn by experience. You have to pick the cat up hundreds of times and inspect his paw a hundred times and have nothing frightening happen before the cat will understand and trust you. The cat must learn through experience that there is nothing to be afraid of, and in fact, that handling is rewarding.

I don't like going to the dentist even if it's just to have my teeth cleaned. But if someone told me that I would get a 500-dollar bill every time I went, I would have the cleanest teeth in town! You can teach your cat to enjoy being picked up, restrained or touched in sensitive areas and actually look forward to these things by associating them with rewards. The rewards you use must be rewards from the cat's point of view. If the cat isn't hungry, then food will not work. If the cat is a little hungry but you use his dry, boring cat food, it will not be viewed as a reward by the cat.

The reward has to be equivalent to a 500-dollar bill. A big, juicy chunk of chicken will probably be enough of a reward to a hungry cat. You know what your cat loves - that's what you use. Kitty must first accept being picked up or whatever handling you're trying to teach him to accept and eventually enjoy, before he gets his favorite treat.

Let's take for example, trying to teach your cat to accept and enjoy having his nails trimmed. And let's suppose the cat goes into a defensive attack mode whenever you hold his paws, much less try to trim his nails.

It is important to start out slowly and gently. Don't

descend on the cat, hold him down, grab his paw, start clipping away, then give him a treat and expect him to learn to like it! Your first goal should be to have a relaxed cat when his paw is just held. Start out by holding a juicy treat in front of kitty - make sure he wants it. Then before you give it to him, slowly reach out and touch his paw very gently for only a second or two.

If your cat wants to jump in your lap for some attention, or wants to play a game, then just before you let him up or start playing, reach out and gently touch his paw. Keep doing this until your cat shows no sign of dislike or resistance. It could take a few trials or it could take a hundred trials over a few weeks. It depends upon the sensitivity of your cat.

The next step would be touching the paw a little longer and maybe even rubbing it just a little before giving your cat the treat. When he is comfortable with this, then you might try gently lifting his paw for a second. When he doesn't mind this anymore, then you can try holding his paw for a few seconds and giving it a gentle massage. By now, if you are doing it right, kitty should think you are pretty weird. "I don't know what's up with the owner, she must have some obsession with my feet, but I think I like it."

Most cats I know tell their owner that it's dinnertime by rubbing up against the refrigerator. Some cats meow at their food bowl. With enough repetitions of the paw handling, your cat might start offering you his paw to signal that it's dinnertime.

Another method you can use to desensitize your cat to handling he dislikes is to find an area of his body that he enjoys having stroked and massaged. Start there and get him nice and relaxed. Slowly, gradually and gently move your hand to his feet. Then immediately return to the areas he loves having rubbed. This way, touching and holding the paws simply becomes part of the massage your cat loves.

Now you can start introducing the nail clippers. Start out by trimming only one nail before giving the cat whatever he likes. Trim only one claw a day and be sure to continue handling his paws throughout the day. If you stop doing the exercises, your cat will forget how rewarding they can be.

The real key here is to progress very slowly. If at any time, your cat resists or doesn't enjoy it, then you're progressing too fast and expecting too much, too soon.

If you force the cat, or it really is unpleasant for him, then he won't be convinced that handling can at least be tolerable if not actually enjoyable. In fact, the training process will go backwards because you will have to start all over again regaining your cat's trust and confidence. Remember, cats learn by experience; so make sure the experience is a good one. It is far better to progress too slowly and succeed, than to go too quickly and fail. Don't force your cat to do anything.

You can apply this method for any activity or handling that your cat doesn't like. Begin to practice now and teach your cat to be handled in ways that might come up later, rather than wait until there's a problem and you have to do something that the cat might not like.

Have Cat, Will Travel

Let's take another example and a common problem that cat owners experience. There are a lot of cats that do not like being put in a carrier.

Usually they associate the carrier with going to the vet or groomer. They put up such a fight, refusing to be put in the box. Instead of waiting until the cat has to visit the vet, then forcing her into an unpleasant event, it's better to accustom the cat to the box now, in a rewarding and non-stressful situation. Set the carrier down somewhere in the house. Let your cat get used to it on her own terms. Let her explore, enter and exit at will. Put her favorite food treats and toys in it and let her discover them. Cats love to hide in boxes and bags and if left to her, your kitty will probably make the carrier a part of her home. When she does, try closing the door on the carrier (when she is inside) for just a second, then open it up again.

Gradually leave the door closed for longer and longer periods of time. Feed kitty in her carrier for a couple of weeks with the door open, then start shutting the door while she is eating. When she is comfortable having the door closed, then try picking the carrier up and setting it back down with kitty inside. Do this several times a day. Then try picking the carrier up and walking across the room. Set it down, open the door and let her out if she wants. Gradually carry her around for longer and longer periods of time before setting the carrier back down again. All the time you're doing this, associate it with rewards and praise.

Once accustomed to the carrier inside the house, put her inside the carrier and take her out to the car. Do this many times before you actually put her in the car. Then, when she is used to being in the car, the next step would be driving around the block, coming back home and letting her out. Then drive around two blocks and so on. Eventually you should be able to drive all the way to the veterinarian's office and she won't be upset at all. Always progress slowly; never start the next step until the cat is completely calm and relaxed in the previous step. Don't punish or yell at her for being frightened, but do not reward her either.

Summary

1. Teach your cat not to bite and scratch you by communicating with him in a way he can understand. If he is too rough when he is playing, let him know you've been hurt and stop the play session.

2. Help your cat vent her playful energy and predatory instincts in ways that are acceptable to you. Provide regular play sessions where she can pounce and attack her toys.

3. If your cat is biting and scratching out of fear and defense, then show kitty by experience that these events are nothing to be afraid of and that in fact, they can be quite rewarding and pleasurable.

8

Fighting

It's normal for any two living beings, whether human, dog or cat, to occasionally have arguments. It's quite common for two or more cats that have been living together to suddenly start fighting. It's unrealistic to expect your cats to get along with each other 100% of the time. When they do have their spats, it is usually best not to interfere. Let them work it out. Anything you do will generally make matters worse. If they have been living together for any length of time, they are probably good friends and they aren't going to try to kill off their best friend! They probably have occasional spats when you aren't home and can't interfere and everything has worked out OK, so it is best to just leave them alone.

Cats are very sensitive and often a fight will start because of something in their environment. Cats that are usually friends can accidentally become temporary adversaries. A common occurrence is when one cat is looking out a window just as a dog passes by. It frightens the cat and he responds by arching his back and hissing. This happens just when the other cat in the house comes strolling by. She doesn't know why her friend is hissing at her, but in turn will hiss back at him. He sees her hiss, doesn't know why and reacts by hissing back at her. A simple case of misunderstanding. Before they know it, they are both mad at each other and neither knows why the other was mad in the first place. Again, give the cats some time, eventually they will work it out and become best of friends again.

If one cat goes to the vet, he often comes back smelling a little different than when he left the house. The cat that stayed home doesn't recognize his friend at first and may react like a new cat has just invaded his territory. The returning cat doesn't understand why he isn't welcome and may react with equal hostility. Again the cats are fighting and we don't understand why. This is normal, and if you leave them alone, they will eventually work it out.

You can help prevent the fighting by wiping down the returning cat with a scent that is familiar to the cat that stayed at home. Use a towel that the stayed-at-home cat has been sleeping on for a few days or any part of his bedding. Or use an article of clothing that has retained your scent. When they greet, both cats will feel more secure when they recognize a familiar scent.

If the fighting does not stop within a reasonable length of time, you may have to start treating the cats like one is a newcomer. Follow the outline of introducing a new cat into the home described in Chapter Two.

Sometimes when you bring a new cat home for the first time and introduce him to your resident cat, things may not always work out. This is because the cat's social structure is so different from ours and different from our other companion pet, the dog.

In the non-domestic setting, cats are usually solitary animals. Emotionally and even physically, they have adapted to solitude. They are designed to be a solitary species. They don't need to be in groups like we do for survival. In fact, cats go to great lengths to be by themselves. They have special avoidance techniques to prevent them from meeting and accidentally running into another cat. This seems strange to us because we are so social. We are also accustomed to our dogs visiting and playing with other dogs and people.

Cats are also extremely flexible and can live quite happily in groups. If presented with group living, they will very often go for it. But some cats won't. This is normal cat behavior.

There is nothing wrong with your cat just because

he would rather be by himself and not become close friends with other cats. You may think your cat is unhappy because he won't become friends with another cat, but that's because we are superimposing our values of happiness on the cat. I know a lot of cat owners who have four or five cats and none of the cats are good friends. They each hang out in their own self-established territories, usually one cat per room in the house. They are all very content and the owner accepts the fact that they will never cuddle and play together. The owner plays with each cat individually and each cat has her own litterbox, toys, scratching post, bedding and dishes. Occasionally the cats encounter each other in the hallway. They will hiss and spit at each other and run back to their own rooms. This is natural behavior for cats and perfectly acceptable to them. The question is whether or not the owner can accept it.

If the cats continuously fight and can't work out a peaceful coexistence; if they actually cause physical harm to each other and it isn't just a ritual of aggressive displays, then it is better to separate them permanently. There is no reason to create unnecessary stress in the cat's life and cause yourself problems. If they are fighting, then they will most likely mark their territories, and cause you other headaches as well. When dogs are living together, they fight to establish their position in the social structure. They need each other because they naturally function as a group. They are social animals. So after a couple of fights, their position is resolved and life goes on. They don't constantly fight and they certainly don't try to inflict real damage to the other. They need each other. But cats don't need each other, so it's possible that they may never stop fighting.

Fortunately, most cats live quite well together. They develop close bonds. They play together and even help care for each other. The best thing you can do is give the cats time and the opportunity to see if they can work things out. They usually do.

9

Booby Traps

Booby traps operate on the principle of superstition. If your cat associates something with an unpleasant experience, he will want to avoid that particular thing in the future. Booby traps should never be designed to cause physical harm or to torment your cat. They are used to discourage a particular behavior your cat indulges in.

Examples

1. If your cat is stealing objects such as clothing from a laundry basket, trash out of cans, food off tabletops or something similar, then a booby trap can effectively stop the behavior. Take a piece of string and tie one end of it to the object your cat will try to steal. Do not use real food on counters or in trash cans. Instead, use a paper towel that has been daubed in tuna oil.

Just something that will attract your cat. In case the booby trap malfunctions, you don't want him to be rewarded for stealing by getting to eat the treat.

Tie the other end of the string to a shake can (an empty aluminum soda can with several pennies in it and taped shut). When the can is shaken, it makes a very loud, obnoxious noise. Set the can down and about a foot away, place another shake can. Place a piece of cardboard on top of these two cans. Now put as many shake cans as possible on the cardboard.

When your cat tries to steal the booby trapped object, the string is pulled and down come all the cans, making a terrible racket. Your call will think the world is crashing down around him and will probably never again approach the object that set it off. Occasionally, the booby trap needs to be set off twice before the cat learns, but usually once is enough.

2. If your cat is jumping up on counter tops, make a false edge to the counter by laying down a piece of cardboard so that 2 or 3 inches protrude over the edge. Weigh down the other edge of the cardboard with shake cans. When your cat's paws hit what he thinks is the counter top edge, it will give way under his paws and a dozen cans will come crashing down around him.

3. If your cat is clawing at certain areas (doors, windows, etc.), try attaching inflated balloons to the area. When claw meets balloon, the sudden burst of air and loud noise will most likely keep your cat away

from the rest of the balloons and therefore the door, window, etc.

4. Once your cat has learned to avoid aluminum cans and balloons, one can or balloon left on the sofa or counter will keep your cat away.

5. Cat don't like their paw pads to stick to surfaces, so two-sided sticky tape put on table tops for a short time often proves useful in keeping cats off tables. It can also be used to make scratching furniture an unpleasant experience.

6. Many cats dislike the feel and sound of aluminum foil. This will often keep them off tables or out of potted plants.

7. Cats hate to snag their claws, so covering objects with netting will help stop your cat from scratching them.

8. Most cats do not like the scent of citrus. Leaving a few fresh orange or lemon peels in taboo areas should help keep the cat away.

9. Check your local pet store or shop online as there are many products available designed as deterrents.

Remember, booby traps should be just severe enough to discourage the activity but never to physically hurt or traumatize your cat. For other ideas on booby traps, refer to the sections on eating plants and scratching furniture.

CPSIA information can be obtained at www.ICGtesting.com
Printed in the USA
BVOW021440010513

319629BV00013B/174/P